MY MAN BLUE

poems *by* Nikki Grimes — pictures *by* Jerome Lagarrigue

Dial Books for Young Readers New York

Published by Dial Books for Young Readers
A division of Penguin Putnam Inc.
345 Hudson Street • New York, New York 10014

Text copyright © 1999 by Nikki Grimes
Pictures copyright © 1999 by Jerome Lagarrigue
Designed by Pamela Darcy
Manufactured in China
First Edition
5 7 9 10 8 6 4

Library of Congress Cataloging in Publication Data
Grimes, Nikki.
My man Blue: poems/by Nikki Grimes; pictures by
Jerome Lagarrigue.—1st ed.
p. cm.
Summary: A collection of poems describes a young boy's life
with his working mother as he establishes a relationship
with his mother's friend Blue.
ISBN 0-8037-2326-1
1. Friendship—Juvenile poetry. 2. Children's poetry, American.
[1. Afro-Americans—Poetry. 2. American poetry.]
I. Lagarrigue, Jerome, ill. II. Title.
PS3557.R489982M96 1999 811'.54—dc21 98-28229 CIP AC

The full-color artwork was prepared using acrylic paint on Canson paper.

For Evan and Bryan Green, two wonderful sources of inspiration.
N.G.

For Lillian and Jean Lagarrigue.
Thanks to "Bam Bam" and Earles Field for having inspired me.
To my entire family and close ones.
J.L.

MY MAN BLUE

His leathery skin's
Like indigo ink
This rugged dude
Who some folk think
Looks fierce in clothes
Of midnight black.
Then there's his teeth:
One gold, three cracked.
And I suppose
The shades could go.
He wears them night
And day, I know.
Still, underneath
This shell, Blue hides
A harmless
Gentle-giant side.

WHEN WE FIRST MET

My mom and me moved here without his help.
So why's this "Blue" guy stop us on the street?
His welcome is on Mom's account, I bet.
I circle, look him up and down and let
Him know his grin's not winning points with me.
My flashing eyes warn "Do not trespass here,"
'Cause in this family *I'm* the only man.
He nods. He understands. So I ease up.
Mom sees me eyeing Blue and lets me know
He's her old friend. It's safe to say hello.
She says they both grew up here way back when.
I mumble, "Well, it's news to me!" But then
I throw my shoulders back and take my stance.
He seems alright. I might give him a chance.

SECOND SON

We're leaning on the stoop, see
counting wedges of blue sky
Sandwiched in between the roofs
and white clouds drifting by.

"Why'd you want my friendship, Blue?"
I blurt out there and then.
"I had a son named Zeke," Blue says.
"These streets became his friend.

"He needed me but by the time
I came, it was too late.
He'd passed the point of trusting his
old man to steer him straight.

"Your missing daddy also left
a hole in you," says Blue.
"If friendship fills it, there's less chance
the streets will eat at you."

"That's cool," I say, all serious.
"But I can't take Zeke's place."
"I know," says Blue. "But your laugh sure
helps conjure up his face!"

FEARLESS

One weekend Blue and me
We storm the park.
I kill time kicking rocks
along the path
while Blue scouts out a tall
and sturdy tree

And urges me to loop
my fear like twine
around a branch and use
the rope to climb.
("Fear's useless otherwise,"
Blue says to me)

"You know I'll be right here
In case you fall."
Believing that is all
it takes to send
me scrambling toward the clouds
the sun, the sky.

      Hey! Climbing's no big deal—
      Next time, I'll fly!

GROUNDED

Asthma stole my
Weekend dose of fun
Left me glum
And wheezing while
The stickball game
Went on as planned
Without me.
I balled my fist
Shook it at the sky
And asked why I was cursed
With lousy breathing.
"Anger is a waste,"
Said Blue. "Use your lips
For something more
Than pouting."

He handed me a hot dog
With the works, said
"Wrap your lips 'round this,
Then tell me if it ain't
The perfect cure
For disappointment."
I rolled my eyes
And could've argued
Easily enough
But my mouth
Was kinda busy
At the time.

THE WATCHER

My favorite ball skipped off the curb
And some dumb kid disguised as me
Ran blindly after it then heard
A tire's skid and spied a rig.
My stubborn feet refused to fly
But Blue reached out and grabbed my belt
And set me on the sidewalk while
The rig reduced my ball to dust.
Blue took my hand and marched me home
Then disappeared without a word.
At times I think Blue's actually
Some gold-toothed angel, guarding me.

DAMON & BLUE

Damon & Blue
Just us two
Cruising up the avenue.

You strut, you glide
But mark our stride
Can't beat us when we're
   side by side.

CLASS BULLY

A bully
kicks me in the knee.
That bully's name
is Tiffany.
I fume
but don't return the blow.
Guys don't hit girls
Blue says, and so
I grab
her wrists 'til she
calms down, while
Laughing
jeering kids stand 'round
and shout "You wimp!" But
they're all wrong.
It's guys
who *don't* hit girls
Who're strong.

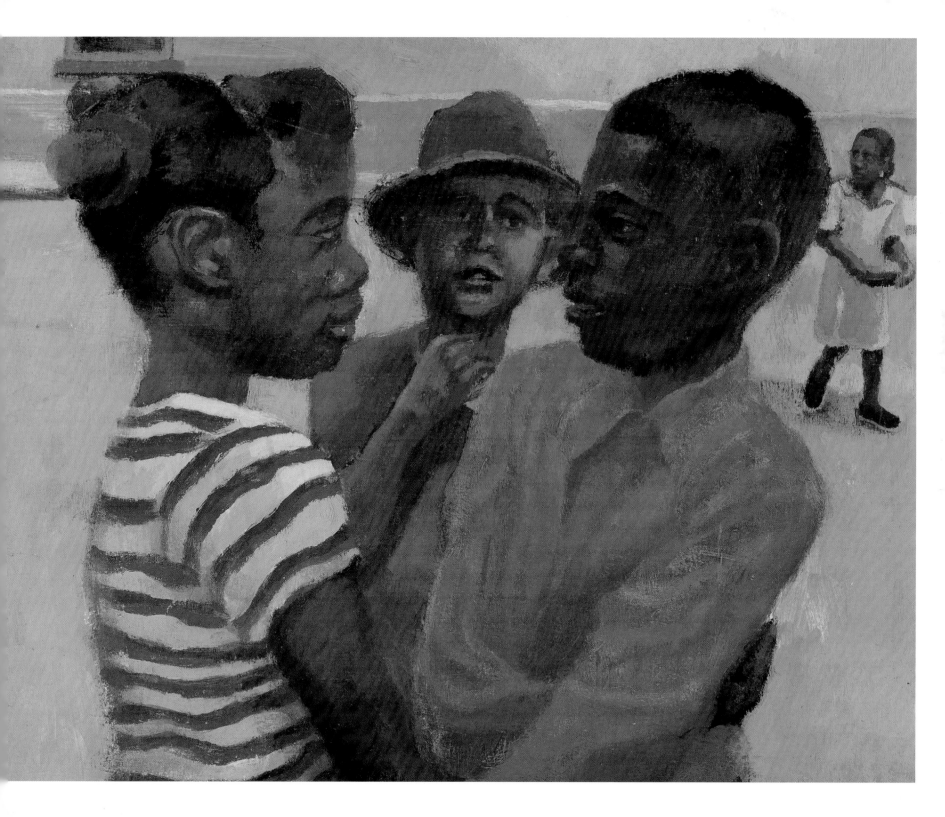

HIS HANDS

His hands
are a rough sculpture
of thick fingers
& thumbs tipped
with work-proud
callouses, his badges
of tough, honest labor
down on the docks.
His hands
are strong stories.
He tells them
sometimes when
I let him hold mine.

ONE-ON-ONE

The game is
Seventeen to four
But scoring
Isn't why we run
And dribble
And jump
While some
Aim guns.
We hit
The hoops
And shoot
For fun.

MY OWN MAN

When Mom works late I wait with busy
hands, pry soup cans open, spread spicy

mustard on rye with lettuce and tomatoes
sliced so thin the cheese peeks through.

It's my Cheddar Deluxe, which Mom loves
better than anything I cook. The boys next

door say, "How's that look? You fixin' supper
like some girl." I shrug off their teasing

and go on pleasing *me*. I read my books,
choose Jazz *and* Rap, and quiet over

chatter. Blue says, "What's the matter
with that?" And, if I take care of my mom

so what? She takes care of me. "Don't be
no Mama's boy," kids say. Well, tough.
                    I'm made this way.

TRAINING SEASON

Blue and me
We spar every day.
Blue fakes a jab
To show me
How it's done.
I don't mind
Since he's the one
Throwing the punches.
He's just trying
To keep me fit
For this world.

THE PLAN

A boy got shot
At school last month.
My knees still knock
At the memory.
What makes somebody
Want to shoot, to kill?
"It's hate," says Blue.
"And fear. One
Holds the gun
While the other
Pulls the trigger.
When you're bigger,
You'll understand."
Well, I don't plan
On hating anyone.
But fear's already
Scratching at my door,
Which means
I got one down
And one to go.
So, Mister Fear,
If you're listening,
You best be leaving
Now.

LIKE BLUE

One day
I'll be like Blue
Not fierce
In black leather
Or built like
A heavyweight
Boxing machine
But like that
Other Blue I've seen
The one who
Says he cares
And shows it.
The one who
Flashes gold
Every time he smiles.